Just Right for Me

By Rose Howell

What do you do with toys you do not need? Read this story to find out what Rob and Lily did.

PEARSON

"What does this paper say?" asked Rob.

"It's about a toy **trade** day," Mom said. She read the paper to Rob and Lily. "Come to the park on Sunday. Bring a toy you don't want. Trade it for something you do want."

"I like all my toys," said Rob.
"I don't want to **trade** any of them."

3

Rob and Lily looked at their toys. Lily said, "These skates are too small! I can trade them. Rob, what will you trade? What do you have that is too small for you?"

Rob looked and looked at his toys. "I don't have anything to trade. I don't have anything that is too small. My toys are all just right," said Rob.

"Here is something," said Lily. "Trade this dog. You have other dogs. You don't need this one. Besides, you are too big for this dog."

6

"No, I still like that dog," said Rob. "I am not too big for it."

"Trade this old truck," said Lily. "You don't need it. You have lots of trucks. Some are newer than this one."

"I still like that truck!" said Rob. "It was my very first truck."

9

 "I am not too big for any of my toys," said Rob. "I have nothing I want to trade."

"Come with me," said Mom. "Let's look at the toys in the hall **closet**."

Rob went to the hall **closet**.
Mom and Lily went, too.

Mom opened the closet.
She took out a small **tricycle**.
"You are much too big for this,"
she said.

"No, I'm not," said Rob.

Rob got on the **tricycle**.
"I am too big for this tricycle!"
he said. "I will trade it!"

On Sunday, Lily took her skates to the park. Rob took his tricycle. Lily found a scooter she liked. Rob found a baseball mitt.

"That mitt is too big for you," said Mom.

"This mitt is too big now," said Rob. "But I will grow into it. Then it will be just right for me!"

Glossary

closet a small room to keep things in

trade to give up one thing and get something in its place

tricycle a riding toy with three wheels